Requiems Of Ghosts

ANVAY SALVE

This book wouldn't have been possible without the people who've always had my back.
Mom & Dad—thank you for believing in me, even when I doubted myself. Your support means everything, and I couldn't have done this without you. A special hug to my sister, who hates hugs. Thanks for sitting with me late at nights to make this dream a reality.

And to the universe—thank you for giving me the words, the creativity, and the chance to put this out into the world.

I'm grateful.

Preface

This book is a collection of thoughts—some borrowed from fleeting moments, others dug up from deep places. Some are loud, some are whispers. Together, they form a journey, not just mine but maybe yours too.

Poetry is strange like that. It turns personal stories into something universal. You might read these words and find a version of yourself hidden between the lines. Or maybe, you'll see something entirely new. Either way, I hope these pages make you pause, reflect, and, if nothing else, feel.

Welcome to this collection. Take what you need from it.

Words From The Author

Poetry has always been a way for me to make sense of the world— its beauty, its chaos, and everything in between. This book isn't just a collection of poems; it's a piece of me. Thank you for reading, for feeling, and for being here.

To the little kid that's still alive inside me who always wanted to do something big,
We made it.

"We don't read and write poetry because it's cute. We read and write poetry because we are members of the human race. And the human race is filled with passion. And medicine, law, business, engineering—these are noble pursuits and necessary to sustain life. But poetry, beauty, romance, love... these are what we stay alive for."

Dead Poets Society

Bloodstained Ardour

Loving you was like pressing my palm to the edge of a knife. The sharp and intruding teeth scarring my rough skin. I knew I was hurting myself, and I still couldn't get enough of it.
And as I watched the blood dripping out from the pierced palm, there was nothing I could wonder about except the fact that the pain felt strangely beautiful. Each throbbing pulse was an "I love you," each sting was proof of how I love you.
The gods screamed at me. I could hear that I should move on, take my hand away from the knife. But how could I? How could I pull myself away from a thing that was so addictive?
And so, I held on. Palm still pressing to the knife, blood still pouring out the wound.

———————— •◦> — <◦• ————————

Fractured Reflections

When we met for the first time, I thought it's me
and you till the end, and maybe even after that.
But now I realised, it was you and me, till we
needed it. So now, I'll leave this all behind,
gather up these broken pieces of us, and frame
it in the living room of my heart.

I Hate Love

The problem is that love hurts me. My soul
loves you more and more each and every day,
against my will. And I can't stop it. I thought
love is supposed to make you happy. Make you
jump and giggle and laugh and whatnot. But
loving you has made this all a burning knife
that's slowly turned inside me.
Against my will.

Wounds heal,
Scars don't.

I stumbled upon your favourite book yesterday.
And I regret perusing the pages of the book,
because as I did so, a picture of us, a picture of
when we were together, landed by my feet. It
was like opening the door in a submerged home.
All the feelings came rushing back, surrounding
me and swallowing me whole. I drowned in
them so deep that I could not breathe anymore.
This time too, you prove me wrong.
Because no matter how big and strong I build
my walls, you'll always be able to bring them
down.

Withered Roses in Paradise

In a garden full of roses, I play love me, love me not.
I stare at the countless bare stems around me,
which said love me, and then I stare at the way
you treated me.
And as I breathe in the land I stand upon, I
realise, I never meant to destroy the garden. But
either way, I ruined it.
And maybe, when I asked God for a way, he
sent me here,
And maybe, this was never about the garden at
all.

————————•❖—❖•————————

The Puzzle
or The Heart?

And everyday, I feel like I woke up in the wrong
world. Because a world where we don't end up
together just doesn't feel right.
A world where we do end up together, would be
just the same. We, fitting each other like jigsaw
pieces. The only difference would be that you
wouldn't be solving a different puzzle.

Lonely
Nights

I stand near the dock, nothing around me
except the fuzzy sky and the bittersweet taste of
your love lingering in the air. I stand there
waiting for you to make your way back to it,
hold my hands in yours, and comfort me in this
solace, assuring me it's going to be alright. I see
you dancing and humming to the sound of the
waves crashing. I didn't notice at first, but now I
can see the silhouette of a person beside you,
holding you ever so dearly. Now the nights have
been left to wonder if I was ever enough.

Lonely Holidays

I woke up this morning and looked at the
calendar to see the holidays approaching. The
excitement is soon replaced by the thoughts of
wanting a home with you. The holidays always
make me realise that I want a home with you.
Not the sadistic type of house. A home. A home
where we, our kids and maybe a dog, live
together. A home where we have our firsts. A
home where we live forever happily. But
unfortunate at love, my heart is going to have
to find shelter in its own house.

So close,
Yet So Far.

I believe that you exist in every version of my
life. In some, we live happily together. In some,
we bloom together. In some, fly together. But
this version of my life will be the most painful of
them all. Because in this version, you will
always be the Sun, and I, the star.

Through the
Eyes of the Phoenix

If I had 3 lives, I'd marry you in 2. And in the
other life, I'd be a writer, writing endless pages
about you, trying to get you back. In the other
life, you'd be the reason I can't sleep at night. In
the other life, I'd be the sand, and you, the
ocean, visiting me from time to time, just to
leave again.

(*Maybe I'm living the third life, at this moment.
Right here right now.*)

I Hope Parallel Universes Exist

And sometimes, I wish it were the opposite.
You write lines about me, while I talk to you
about other girls.
You mourn, while I dance gleefully.
You be the moonlight, while I become the
sunflower.
Your words forming a world I could never
reach.

And maybe in another universe, I'll give you a
nickname.
In another universe, you'll be the solution to my
pain.
Maybe in another universe, falling in love with
you won't be a crime.
In another universe, I'll get to call you mine.

Dry Oceans

I think I'm okay, until on a random Tuesday
afternoon when it all comes flooding back.
Your face, your touch, the scent of your
perfume.
Everything hits me in the stomach hard. So
hard, that I'm falling and can barely get up.
But the hardest hit of them all was the way you
grew distant and acted like you never cared.

For I could swim a thousand miles, but the
silence between us will always leave me dry.

Beneath The
Surface

I care about you, even if we never speak again.
I care about you, even when I say I don't want
you anymore.
I care about you, even when you said you hate
me,
I care about you, even when I don't.

I Hate Every Day

I hate the morning because now it doesn't
include your "good morning" texts.
I hate the afternoon because it drags along
without your smile.
I hate the evening because the night approaches,
And I hate the night because I drown in the
hollow memories.

Silent Screams

I missed you today.
I missed you today, but I did it quietly. So
silent, that nobody noticed.
Oh, but how I felt it. How I felt the absolute
pain of you leaving, in my heart. I almost felt it
as if I was as important to you as you were to
me.

I missed you quietly today, but it felt so loud.

A Healer For A Healer

I think of myself as a healer,

people heal and they leave.

But who heals the healer?

Who's Adam without Eve?

Because, I've always wondered at night

What the purpose of my life was

But now, I guess, it's clear as daylight

All I get to say is "don't worry of what was"

Obviously, not the words of affirmation,

Even though it'd be as simple as cup art,

Because maybe if I did actually say them,

The whole world would fall apart.

But I don't mind being single,

Although sometimes I have these glimpses in my head,

That I'm being loved and mingled,

And served with breakfast in bed.

Though I mend the hearts of others,

And offer comfort in their pain,

Under the thick covers,

I too, wish for the same.

Roses and Thorns

You gave me roses. The only thing I couldn't understand is that if the red on the roses was love, with its warmth and passion, or blood, hinting at pain and suffering. Each petal seemed to carry a different meaning. Some Crimson, while others, a deep Garnet. This bouquet is a riddle, each petal hinting at a different story, each thorn poking the hidden truth.

Which story do you want me to believe?

*Unravelled
By You*

How can I know each crevice of yours, the story
of every scar you have, the touch of your skin,
and still walk past you, pretending I never
wondered if our daughter would have your
eyes? How can I cross paths with you, as if the
sight of your face doesn't make my heart skip a
beat? How can I remember your laugh echoing
through the silence of the night, the warmth of
your embrace, and still pretend I don't
remember every little detail of you?
How can I silence the longing of closing the
void between us, and ask if you ever felt the
same?

Muse
Of Midnights

I wish you were nothing more than a face in the
crowd. But instead,
You're the thought that keeps me up at night.
You're the muse of everything I write.
You're the light in my life that shines so bright.
You're the scenery everyone dies to have in their
sight.
You're the love I hold onto so tight.

A House Is Not A Home

And just as I am about to move on, my heart
digs out the little sonnets I wrote for you from
the back of my mind, when you would sit and
stare at me, love in your eyes, blush on your
cheeks. And I realise, I am not even close to
moving on. In fact, after all this time, I might
still be in the same place. I just wish that this
place was the same place 3 years ago, when this
broken house was a happy home, and this
heart, a whole piece.

Sand Of Tears

And I stand there, unable to move, as the
realisation sets in, that you're no longer mine.
I watch you from afar, happier than you were
with me. I try to hold onto the last bit of love
that you left me with, but it, too, is slipping
through my fingers, just like small grains of
sand, through the small hands of a child.
It started raining, I didn't realise, but maybe
this time, the world does not want me to cry
alone.

*Am I a
mirror?*

I wasn't ready for you to leave me. They say
time heals, that I'll forget you in no time, but 4
years later, I'm still here, dancing to our song,
Imagining you're here with me, playing your
favourite songs on the guitar, picturing you
appreciating me. 4 years later, there's still a hole
in my heart, and you are still, the final puzzle
piece.
I wasn't ready for you to leave me, but now,
you've turned into one of them, and I, into you.

Crossroads

We were like January and December, just a
moment away, but a lifetime apart.
Like intersecting lines, destined to meet only for
a second, and then diverging again forever.
Like stars in a constellation, near enough to
touch, but a world apart.
Just like winter fades into spring, our paths
touched, only to drift into different seasons of
life.

Quiet
Revenge

And I'll simply just walk away. Wanting no
revenge. For one day, your son will sit in his
room, tears streaming down his cheek
uncontrollably, his hands trembling while
wiping the tears with the back of his hand. And
the weight of you knowing you once caused
such pain will stay with you forever, like a
shadow. And that will be my quiet revenge.

Favourite Colour For
A Favourite Person.

You said your favourite colour was red.

So I bleed for you

Just so I could know

What it would feel like

To be your favourite.

Worth All The Pain?
Worth All The Trouble?

I tell my friends that I moved on and I don't
care anymore. But I still think of you when that
particular song plays. When that Ice-cream
truck passes by. When the little birds gather
around as somebody feeds them seeds. When I
see a thing as simple as a black scrunchie lying
on the receptionist's table. Because the truth is,
I miss you. I miss you every passing second,
every passing hour and I can't stop.

But you seem fine without me,
So is it worth missing you?

A Study That
Won't Exist

They say it takes 21 days to break a habit. But
it's been 3 years and I still love you. Because
you weren't a habit, you were an addiction. And
I don't think there's any study to show how long
it takes to get over an addiction. Even if there
is, it won't work for me. Because you are
someone, which I can't forget, can't replace, and
can't do anything with.

All I do is Wonder,
All I do is Wander.

I wonder what happens
When you hear my voice,
Do you keep listening like you used to,
Or brush it off saying "I got other boys."

I wonder what happens
When you hear our song,
Do you turn off the radio,
Or do you think of us all along?

I wonder what happens
When you hear my name,
Do you laugh at the stupidity,
Or does your mind go insane?

I hope whatever happens
Time heals the threatening maim,
While I keep weeping
In this sorrowful champagne.

One Truth,
Countless Lies.

And you said you could never say goodbye.

And that's maybe

The only thing you were truthful to,

Because you left,

And I'll never know why.

The Rain
Started Pouring

The rain started pouring
I remember the night we met,
When you said that you loved me,
Words, as lovely as the roses of death.

The rain started pouring,
Each drop having weight,
While I'm lost in a maze of heartbreak
Searching for a way.

The rain started pouring,
My soul denying to forget each day,
Because you're the melody in my heart,
That won't fade away.

The rain started pouring,
While my heart is at war,
It craves for just a single thing,
Your caressing touch, once more.

Broken House

"I want to go home." I said, forgetting that my
home doesn't exist anymore.
My home, with a laugh that healed a torn heart,
with lips, as sweet as a gentle breeze on a
summer day, with arms, in which I could spend
my entire life in, with a voice, of which even a
nightingale was jealous of, was gone.
 And now I was homeless.
"I want to go home." I said, but this time, I had
to build the house from fragmented memories.

More Than Friends,
Less Than Lovers.

The phone buzzes in my pocket. It's my friend asking me if me and her talk anymore. I send a "no we don't". I type "we're just friends" but don't friends get along together? I delete it and say "She's like an acquaintance" but an acquaintance is someone whom you don't know much. And I knew her very well. From her favourite show, to her go-to starbucks order, I knew her.

So, the question was, what are we?

We were more than acquaintances. More than friends. More than friends, but not lovers. So then, what are we?

What do you call people who knew each other so well at one point?

People who used to talk to each other every second of the day?

People, who were in love, but never together. What are they?

*Patios
At 3am*

I wish pain felt as beautiful as poetry made it
sound. But all I feel are the lonely teardrops
slowly falling from my face, glimmering in what
little light of hope is in front of me, that you'll
still return, even though my brain says you
won't.
But what's a heart that won't fight for a love it
longs for?
What's a sunflower without a sun to follow?
What's a dock without a ship?
What's a song without a tune?
What am I, without you?

April:
The Month Of Waiting

It's the month of April again.

Soon, it will be August,

And soon enough, it will be December.

April will come again,

But you won't be here with me.

But that's alright,

I'll still wait for you,

When April comes again.

Scorched
Silence

We dreamt together about warmth, so I let myself burn. I lit myself on fire, so I could keep us warm. I burnt all the skin I had, just so you could feel my bones. Because for just once in my life, I would like to be understood. I would like to talk to someone, just as I talk to myself when no one is around.

Want vs Need,
You vs Me.

You were everything I wanted,
But I couldn't have you.
I was everything you needed,
But you didn't want me.

Nothing And Everything
At The Same Time

Was it all really that easy? To push everything away? To pretend we were nothing more than two leaves on a tree? Than two roses in a bouquet? Was it really that easy as you showcase it, or are you cast as the actor in the little demonic play called 'life'? Are we playing the same act, where we both love someone, just not each other? Because the least I know, you love him more. He's more to you than I ever was, and ever will be. He's nothing I want to be like, and yet, everything I want to be.

So tell me, was it really that easy?

Ashes Turned
To Stone

I almost turned into dust, until I met you. You
came in my life and saved me like one of the
superheroes. You caught me when I was falling
off of a building, swam miles when I was
drowning, stood in the way of the bullet coming
at me. You were my superhero. You were mine.
Words in any language can't convey the feeling
I felt when you said you couldn't save me
anymore. It was like feeling nothing and
everything at the same time.
I almost turned into dust, and you turned me
into a boulder. Now I don't know how to
break. I don't know how to be dust again.

Everything and Nothing

I wish I could turn you back into a stranger.
But then again, aren't you already one?
Now you've become one of the people I see in
the streets, who I know nothing about. I don't
know what goes on in your day, what you do,
what's your favourite movie, or anything.
Now, you're just somebody that I used to know.
A familiar stranger. That's all. And I think I'll
find happiness in that. Because even though
you're a stranger, you're at least familiar.
For if we ever cross paths again, a single nod is
all I'll need to understand a thousand words.

If Only…

If only my heart were as cold as it pretends to
be,
I could get over this.
If only my words were better than "maybe it's
my fault",
I could get over this.
If only my thoughts would stop making me cry
every night,
I could get over this.
If only I loved you a little less every day,
I could get over this.

———————— •◦• — •◦• ————————

1 is greater than 2.

In school, they taught me how 2 is the greater
digit when it's beside 1. I did always believe that
they were right.

Until the day I stood next to him.

I no longer felt great being second to your one.

I Don't Want To Wake Up.

I still wake up with things to tell you. And
hopefully, one day, I won't.
I won't remember your voice, nor your face. It
would just be a faded memory.
And I don't know how to feel about that.
I don't know how to feel about anything
anymore. Maybe the last thing I felt was the
feelings I had for you, and you threw it away
like it was nothing.
Maybe that's what broke me. Shattered me. But
you don't care, right? You didn't mean it when
you said you would be here with me in my
darkest times. Dumb of my heart to think that
you were speaking the truth.
But who is my heart to blame? It always stuck
to its words. Because the least I know, even at 3
am, if you called me crying, I would pick up in
less than a second.

But one day, I won't. One day, I won't have
things to tell you.

Strangers
Once More

We haven't talked in a few fortnights,
Does it feel like something new?
Are you getting used to the surrounding?
Am I the only one bruised?

Do you search for my voice,
Like how my heart seeks for yours,
Does your heart scream my name,
Like I'm your only lost cause?

I can't sleep at night,
Because my mind always thinks about you,
And all it does is,
Break my heart in two.

It was better if we stayed
Strangers as before,
It seems like you moved on,
But you're my heart's only core.

Wilted Trust

The flowers are blooming again, but there's no
scent. The scent which used to make a man full
of dolefulness, light up with joy. The scent
which healed even a melancholy soul.
Maybe that's what happens when you pluck a
flower. It doubts even the most innocent and
caring bee.

The flowers are blooming again, but this time,
the petals droop with the weight of pensiveness,
denying the bees even a little bit of nectar.

A Rain That Longs To Bloom

And then,

I became the rain in your night sky.

A thorn in your rose.

A chainsaw in your forest.

But how could I ever tell you that,

You were the sugar in my coffee?

The water in my desert?

The paint on my canvas?

How could I ever tell you that you were the
only thing I'd ever beg for?

Writers Love Paper,
The Way I Love You.

People become writers when there's nobody to
listen.
When the feelings inside their heart are trying to
climb out, overflowing, overwhelming, and still,
they can't think of a person who would care
enough to listen.
So they write. They write and write, until the
blood in their fingers bleed upon the paper.
A paper would always listen to what they have
to say.

Darkened
Heartaches

I always hope she talks back on the other side

when I talk to you,

Laying on a field or a leafy road or a grassy

ground,

But where is the other side

when you aren't around?

Without you everything goes calm,

Except my heart always pounds,

With noone to talk to of her,

I can't help but break down.

———————— •◆▷ — ◁◆• ————————

~~Friends And Lovers~~
A Friend, And A Lover.

You were a galaxy to me, while I was a star for
you.
You were a sculpture to me, while I was a
pebble for you.
You were a garden for me, while I was a petal
for you.
You were everything I wanted, while I was just
another person for you.

———— •◆ — ◆• ————

The Chosen One

I look at the clock, time slowly passing, the sun slowly rising, and I'm still wondering what it's like to be chosen. Because I was never chosen, I was always a maybe, sometimes probably, but never definitely.

Never the chosen one.

Where'd All The Time Go?

I think it's unfair how everybody gets a piece of
you but me. How this love is so silent, but once
it used to scream.
It's funny how you said you'd die without me,
and now when we're actually apart, you didn't
even flinch a bit.
 And I hate how my heartbeat drops when I
hear your voice, the same voice that I needed to
start my day.

I think it's unfair how everybody gets a piece of
you but me.
Unfair, because I used to have the most of you
and now, not even the least.

Another Girl?
Absolutely Not.

"She was just another girl. Forget her."
If she was just another girl, why do my eyes cry
every time I think of her?
If she was just another girl, why does my heart
ache when I hear her name?
If she was just another girl, why do I look for a
falling star everytime I'm out just so I could
wish about her?
If she was just another girl, why is she the first
and the last thought of my day?
If she was just another girl, why are my friends
tired of hearing her name? If she was just
another girl, why do I pray for her everyday?

I *wish* she was just another girl.

At least that way, I wouldn't cry myself to sleep
every night thinking about her.

All Over Again

I saw a boy crying across the street. When I
asked him what was wrong, he hugged me
tightly and cried, "she was everything to me. It
couldn't have been better till it ended." I console
him while my heart reminds me of you, of how I
cried to my friends that I couldn't live without
you, of how I couldn't sleep without your good
night text for nights, of all the love and
affection. I returned to my home, and now, I'm
15 again, in the dorm room, crying over you.
15 again, healing from someone I once thought
I would heal with.

Mamihlapinatapai

There is a word in an indigenous language
meaning, a look shared by two people who
want to initiate something, but that neither will
start.
When I read about this for the first time, I
thought about you. Always friends, never
lovers. Neither of us pushed for more. Always
asking for advice when life seemed to break
down, wiping away each other's tears when
someone left us broken.
We would laugh together, cry together, heal
together, but never *be* together. And I think
we've both wondered why, and yet, have no
answer for it.
So tonight, I'll settle for whatever you offer.
But once, just once, my heart
would like to linger in the unspoken space,
tasting what could be.

Chocolate Makes Me Happy

I say that I am over you but I still look for you
in every room that I'm in.

In fact, even a room filled with people feels
empty without your presence.

Now, in every room I'm in, may it be a
restaurant, or a bachelor's party, I still keep a
seat empty beside me like I used to earlier, but
this time, only to hope that you'll sit by me and
tell me it's going to be okay.

But since you're not here in this coffee shop, I'll
sit alone, hang my coat on the empty chair
beside me, and order your favourite hazelnut
chocolate, while I drown in our memories.

Warmth In Winter

I learned a new word today.

Apricity.

It's a noun used to define the warmth of the sun
in winter. And maybe, it can be used to describe
a person.
But can everyone use it?
Does everyone have a person who feels like the
sun in winter?
Like a cup of hot chocolate after a heavy
rainstorm?
Like a comforting embrace on a cold night?
Like a familiar melody that soothes the soul?
The word exists, but where's the person?
Where's the person I could call my apricity?

Embracing
Ghosts

And sometimes, in these lonely nights, there is this silent little urge to fit in your arms once again. To feel the warmth of your breath, the gentle rise and fall of your chest as you do so. To play with the strands of your hair that hold the scent that is now etched in my memory. But then, I have to wave you goodbye and open my eyes and realise the space beside me is still empty. As a hollow piece of wood. So, I grab a pillow, and hold you close through these isolated nights.

About The Author

Anvay Salve is a 16-year-old poet who writes like his therapist charges per metaphor. In reality, he just has a very dramatic heart, and a knack for turning emotional chaos into art.

Requiems of Ghosts is his debut collection—a rollercoaster of emotions that dips into heartbreak, identity crises, and that weird in-between feeling of being too much and not enough at the same time. He thinks it's the poetic equivalent of crying in your room at 2 a.m., but in a beautiful, cathartic way.

When he's not writing poetry, Anvay can be found playing his guitar and honing his singing skills. He is a passionate reader, has represented his school and college at the district level in football and basketball. Anvay loves working relentlessly to embellish his versatile personality.

He believes sadness is temporary, but poetry? That's forever. Especially if you put it in a book and sell it.

Get To Know Me More

@_anyway_anvay

salveanvay@gmail.com